Toya L. Poplar

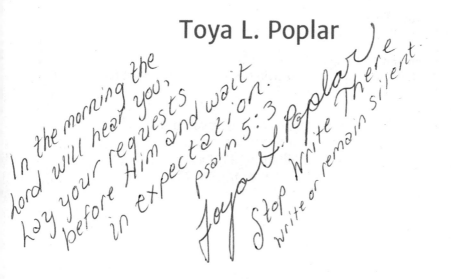

In the morning the
Lord will hear you,
Lay your requests
before Him and wait
in expectation.
Psalm 5:3

Toya L. Poplar

Stop Write There.
Write or remain silent.

STOP WRITE THERE

DEDICATION

Maegan White, thank you for inspiring me to keep fighting the good fight of faith. When I look at your life, I get a glimpse of God's glory. Your friendship is a treasure that I will cherish forever.

"You see, the short-lived pains of this life are creating for us an eternal glory that does not compare to anything we know here."

2 Corinthians 4:17 VOICE

This book is dedicated to people like me. Creative Christians who feel as if a major part of who they are is starting to die because they spend more time pretending to be normal than they do pursuing their passion. The modern day David. The dreamers like Joseph. Those who can identify with Martha's madness, but crave Mary's gladness. The widow who does not know the value of her mites. The Hannah whose weariness is mistaken for wickedness. The Vashti and the Esther. The Sarah who awaits God's promise and doesn't want to birth an Ishmael in the process.

If you are more than just a lover of words, but a lover of The Word, this book is for you. If you feel as though every force in Hell is attempting to silence you and convince you that it is too late for you to create, I dedicate this book to you. The struggle is real but God is greater.

Whatever you find to do, do it well because where you are going-the grave-there will be no working or thinking or knowing or wisdom.
Ecclesiastes 9:10 VOICE

CONTENTS

STOP WRITE THERE

ACKNOWLEDGEMENTS

I would like to acknowledge my Lord and Savior, Jesus Christ. Thank you for directing my path and encouraging me to use what is in my hand. Melvin Poplar Jr., my husband, my hero, my friend. There are no words to express my gratitude for your support. Your love towards me is a perfect illustration of how Christ gave Himself for His bride. To my older children Melvin, Trinity and Amiya, thank you for making me look like I know what I'm doing as a parent. Your creativity inspires me. To my younger children Nehemiah, Jaden and Reginald, you rock my world and I am eternally grateful that God would allow us to grow together. When He rerouted your destiny He rewrote my heart's story and I am enjoying our happily ever after.

I must acknowledge some of my favorite writers, cleanest streams & greatest givers. To the ladies who eagerly agreed to edit the overflow of my heart; your sisterhood is invaluable. Thanks for being key players on my dream team. My childhood friends that I am privileged to have relationships with. My college buddies who will remain friends for life. To family members who have encouraged me to shine since I was young and remind me of how much I am my father's child. To all my favorite rhymers from Rhymers for the Lord, you sharpen me. To Marriage More Abundantly, I am thankful that God knit our hearts together. To the Proverbial Girls in my world, you enhance my virtue. Hidden in Him, Second Mile, My Sister's House, W.O.V.E.N., Our City on a Hill, Write Out, Winning Women, THRIVE and Freedom Writers when I say "I love you to life," I really mean it. To the spiritual moms and mentors that I have met along the way, you know who you are and what you have done, and I am eternally grateful. To my father Joseph Burton, I am grateful for the love you showed and seeds you sowed; my heart is set on Heaven because of the impact you made while on earth. Last but certainly not least, I must acknowledge my itty-bitty Mama, Madelyn Joyce Spearman. The older I get, the more "I get" you. Thank you for loving me well.

"Don't let loyalty and faithfulness leave you.
Bind them on your neck;
Write them on the tablet of your heart."
Proverbs 3:3 CEB

1. WRITE OR REMAIN SILENT

Sometimes we find ourselves having to choose between cultivating our passion and being "productive". Stop Write There was created to challenge you to do both. Our fast paced culture tends to associate creativity and rest with laziness. I have noticed that productivity is empowered by taking the time to cultivate creativity and get adequate rest. Even in the smallest of ways, DO WHAT YOU LOVE. If you are a creative person and find yourself constantly suppressing creativity, you will start to feel as though a part of you is dying. What you feel will become real because WHAT YOU FEED WILL GROW AND WHAT YOU STARVE WILL DIE.

"Whatever you find to do, DO IT WELL because where you are going- the grave—there will be no working or thinking or knowing or wisdom."
Ecclesiastes 9:10 (VOICE)

Create, work, and plan while you can. None of us is promised tomorrow. If we want to hear "well done," then it would do us well to DO WELL. Stop procrastinating and start writing today.

Sometimes, we lose sight of who we are. I often joke with my friends about what I call "The Curse of Creativity." When the devil begins to use the art of suggestion to make us question who we are, it is easy for our minds to concoct motion picture movies that make us believe that his lies are true.

There is a story in I Samuel Chapter 30 in which David and his men lost their wives, children, and possessions. They were so discouraged that they cried until they had no strength to cry. David was in a dark place. His possessions had been burned, family taken captive, and the people he was with wanted to stone him. David's response was exceptional; the Bible tells us that David encouraged himself. What may have been David's worst defeat led to a great victory as he encouraged himself. David was a creative person and I can only imagine the mental battles he fought. Just think, one of his wives despised the way he danced. Saul threw daggers at him as he worshipped. Some of the most profound psalms ever written were composed by David during some of his most difficult seasons. I have faith that just as David encouraged himself, prayed to God, overcame the enemy, and watched God's restoration process take place in his life, so can you. I Samuel 30:18 says David recovered all that was stolen from him.

Have you ever found an old notebook that contained goals or dreams that you once dreamed back when you dared to believe that dreams come true? Well, dreams still come true. Even if you have stopped living and have settled for existing, it is my prayer that you will dream again, believe again, and write again. This journal is an opportunity to reflect on what is left so that you don't have to lament over the time that has been lost. If you are currently cultivating creativity, KEEP GOING! The world needs to see a glimpse of The Creator's creativity at work within you.

Life is too short to go on pretending that you are someone you are not. Your life matters, so live it fully. You have a voice, so share truth in love. You are not who you once were; you have been made new. It is time for the world to meet who you are becoming, no introduction necessary. Just grab your pen and your bible, and "do you." Being real doesn't mean being real carnal. Being real is simply choosing not to violate your divine design. If you are presently walking through darkness, SHINE. If your life's soundtrack has come to a screeching halt, SING. If everything around you seems to be the same, CHANGE. You were created to CREATE! God breathed life into you so that you can BREATHE life into others so stop holding your breath. START WRITE HERE!

2. CHANGE

I washed my van and it looked like new.
I organized my home and it grew larger.
I saved some money and felt more secure.
I detoxed my body and it cleansed my soul.
I overcame my fears and my dreams grew larger.
I examined my past and foresaw my future.
I bridled my tongue and befriended wisdom.
I embraced my flaws and discovered my beauty.
In hindsight, all that really changed was my perspective.

Sometimes I don't need to hear something new. I just need to be reminded of something true. How about you?

I can change my vehicle, home, financial status, body, car, job, house, church, or spouse and still struggle with the same things. However, if I change my perspective, my life will change even if everything around me remains the same. Take note, changing the latter is much easier than the former. Make the necessary changes today. Change your perspective and your life will follow.

"Finally, brothers and sisters, fill your minds with beauty and truth. Meditate on whatever is honorable, whatever is right, whatever is pure, whatever is lovely, whatever is good, whatever is virtuous and praiseworthy."
Philippians 4:8 VOICE

Date: _____

What are some areas in which you feel as though you have lost sight of the truth? What are some necessary changes you would like to see take place in your life?

Truth is the key to being free!

"EASE me down the path of Your truth.
FEED me Your word because You are the True
God who has saved me. I wait all day long,
hoping, trusting in You."
Psalm 25:5 Voice

3. PROCRASTINATION

"If you want your dreams to come true, don't oversleep."
-Yiddish Proverb

"He who runs from God in the morning will scarcely find Him
throughout the rest of his day."
-John Bunyan

God knows which seeds will grow and if you never plant, you will
never know. What are you waiting for? Stop waiting for the perfect
conditions to do what God has placed in your heart.

"Those who watch and wait for favorable winds never plant, and
those who watch and fret over every cloud will never harvest. Get
up early to sow your seed, and in the evening find worthwhile things
to do, for you never know which will profit you-maybe this, maybe
that, maybe both." Ecclesiastes 11:4 & 6 VOICE

"God Says I Can"

My flesh says, "Be fake."
God says, "Be real."
My heart says, "I'll break."
God says, "I'll heal."
Emotions say, "I'll faint."
God says, "Just stand."
Satan says, "I can't."
God says, "I can."

"I can do all things through Christ who strengthens me."
Philippians 4:13

Date: _____

What are some areas in which you are procrastinating? Faithful farmers rise early and rest well when the sun goes down. How can you carve out time in the early morning and use time more wisely in the evening to plant, water or nurture your goals?

God says you can.

4. FORGOTTEN

Have you ever felt like the people you helped forgot about helping you? Imagine what Joseph felt like as he sat in prison and watched the cupbearer be restored to his position after he interpreted his dream.

> "But I ask you one thing. Remember me when things are going well for you. If you have the opportunity, do me a favor and mention me to Pharaoh. Perhaps he will get me out of this place.
>
> Sadly the chief cupbearer did not remember Joseph at this time, instead, he forgot all about him." Genesis 40: 14 & 23 VOICE

Joseph's journey is found in Genesis 37:1-50:26

If you are already familiar with the favor that was upon Joseph's life, then you know The Father did not forget him. In fact, it was God that caused the cupbearer to remember him at the moment that Pharaoh needed someone to interpret his dream. Had the cupbearer remembered Joseph before his gift was needed, it would not have mattered to Pharaoh and Joseph would have remained in prison. God not only remembered Joseph, but he rewarded him in a remarkable way. Joseph became a wise leader who sharpened his skills while serving as both a slave and a prisoner.

Maybe your family mocked you for being a dreamer or refused to recognize the gift that is inside of you. Ask God to help you to forgive and forget the pain of the past so that you can focus on being fruitful in the present. There may be times in which you feel forgotten, but have faith! The Father sees and will be faithful to bring you full circle.

17

Date: _____

Reflect on a time in which your gift benefited others around you as you wrestled with feeling forgotten. Your gift will eventually make room for you. In the meantime, be sure you are making room for your gift! Instead of focusing on feeling forgotten, focus on The Father and how He is faithful to see what man forgets.

Read Genesis 41:51 & 52

Why would Joseph name his sons Manasseh and Ephraim?

Look up the meaning of their names to understand the significance to Joseph's life. Forgetting a painful past can prepare you for a fruitful future.

God sees what man forgets.

"For God is not unjust to forget your work and labor of love which you have shown toward His name, in that you have ministered to the saints, and do minister."

Hebrews 6:10 NKJV

5. Used

Have you ever been in a class and said the correct answer to a question quietly, only to have another student say the answer aloud, because they heard you whisper it? Did you feel cheated? I think one of the most frequent games that the enemy plays with creative people is to make them think that someone is trying to steal their ideas and share them before they can. Have you ever felt like people were using you just to steal your ideas?

What if God is using you? If God has gifted you to be a teacher to those who teach, counselor to those who counsel, and an inspiration to those who inspire, then do not let the devil trick you into believing that everyone is out to use you. The truth is, God could be using you to supply wisdom to the body of Christ. If you have spiritual knowledge, the entire body is edified when you share wisdom and insight with others. If you are one who deliberately steals other's ideas, enjoy your few moments of fame because scripture says that is all you have.

> "For whoever has [spiritual knowledge], to him more will be given and he will be furnished richly so that he will have abundance; but from him who has not, even what he has will be taken away."
> Matthew 13:12 AMP

> "Surely, no matter what you are doing (speaking, writing or working), do it all in the name of Jesus our Master, sending thanks through Him to God our Father."
> Colossians 3:17 VOICE

> "One shares liberally and yet gains even more, while another hoards more than is right and still has need."
> Proverbs 11:24 VOICE

Date: _____

Prior to reading Chapter 5, did you consider yourself a vessel of inspiration being used by God? Or did you see yourself as a puppet being used by man?

Name a person or group of people that you consider "safe places" to share ideas, insight and spiritual revelation.

God designed the body to work with one another,
not compete against each other.

6. COMPARISON

All creative minds know how comparison corrupts creativity. Any time that I start to compare myself to someone else, I contemplate quitting. A strategy to combat discouragement is to find joy in encouraging others. It takes courage to encourage, as any coward can compete. (No offense to all the competitive people who might be reading this.)

Competition is not a bad thing when you compete against yourself. For example, if you are a runner and you compete against your former running time, a faster time means that you are getting stronger and your entire body benefits from your progress. When we set personal goals and obtain them, the entire body is edified. God designed the body to work in conjunction with one another. There is no need for my neck to compete with my knees. Every part of my body has a specific role to play and each one is significantly important.

"That there should be no division in the body; instead, all parts mutually depend on and care for one another. If one part is suffering, then all the members suffer alongside it. If one member is honored, then all the members celebrate alongside it. You are the body of the Anointed, the Liberating King; each and every one of you is a vital member." I Corinthians 12:25-27 VOICE

Don't be jealous or proud, but be humble and consider others more important than yourselves.
Philippians 2:3 CEV

Date: _____

Reflect on a time in which your motivation to do something was driven by a desire to compete.

Write about a gift you have that perfectly complements someone else's.

Do you see the difference?

If your motives are pure, then your motivation will be also.

7. CHOOSE LOVE

You might be wondering, "What if I have been used, misused, disregarded and stolen from in the name of creativity?" My advice would be to choose love. In Luke 17:32 when Jesus told the disciples to "remember Lot's wife," it wasn't a question, it was imperative. The only way we can move forward towards what the future promises, is to stop allowing the pain from our past to paralyze us.

"Most of all, love each other steadily and unselfishly, because love makes up for many faults." I Peter 4:8 VOICE

"Choose Love"

Love covers and prevails.
It protects and does not fail.
It forgives, it lets go.
Love waters and makes things grow.
Love is patient. Love is kind.
Love forgets and does not remind.
Love is not jealous.
Love has no conceit.
When we choose to love there is no defeat.
Love is easier to say than it is to do.
Love is effortless when it is true.
A Christian with no love sounds absurd,
Because love's actions speak louder than our words.

Date: _____

Read I Corinthians 13:1-3

Write I Corinthians 13:4-8

Recite the following words out loud:

"I can have a way with words and if my words are not laced with grace and led by love, it will be irritating to the hearer. I can forecast the future, be perceptive and have mountain moving faith, but if I lack love, I am nothing. I can be the greatest giver and do selfless acts but if it is not motivated by love, it does not mean anything."

Love always wins because Love never fails.

8. EVERY TIME

You may say with your mouth that you have forgiven someone, but your actions will reveal if your words are sincere. Maybe you have been hurt more than once by the same individual and you find yourself asking the same question Peter asked,

"Lord, when someone has sinned against me, how many times ought I forgive him? Once? Twice? As many as seven times?" Jesus replied, "You must forgive not seven times, but seventy times seven."

Matthew 18:21-22 VOICE

Isn't it fascinating that Peter would be the one to ask Jesus this question regarding forgiveness, since he was the disciple to declare that he would never deny Christ? (Matthew 26:31-35) Peter later did the very thing he said he would not do. (Denied Christ). Peter found himself in need of the same forgiveness he pondered withholding from someone else. It is important for us to forgive every time because of the mercy that God has shown us. You can never go wrong while choosing to do what's right.

"Every Time"

I will not be dismayed.
My God cannot fail.
Our Lord was betrayed so that love would prevail.
I choose love because Love first chose me.
I choose to forgive because Love set me free.
I choose to forget because no matter the crime,
When God looks at me He sees Christ, every time.

If someone claims, "I love God," but hates his brother or sister, then he is a liar. Anyone who does not love a brother or a sister whom he has seen, cannot possibly love God, whom he has never seen. I John 4:20 VOICE

Date: _____

If you really love God then you should love mercy. Look up the word "mercy" write the definition below. Now read the antonym for the word "mercy" and ask yourself which words describe you?

Read Micah 6:8. What does God require of us?

"So live your life in such a way that acknowledges that one day you will be judged. But the law that judges also gives freedom, although you can't expect to be shown mercy if you refuse to show mercy. But hear this; mercy always wins against judgment! Thank God!"
James 2:12 & 13 VOICE

"He has shown you, O man, what is good; and what does the LORD require of you but to do justly, to love mercy, and to walk humbly with your God?"
Micah 6:8 NKJV

9. FORGIVENESS

People who forgive quickly are often those who know what it is like to need forgiveness. Therefore, they love deeply and extend forgiveness freely. It is similar to grace... Those people who extend little grace are those who have not needed it (or recognized their need for it). Then there are others, who know they do not deserve God's grace so they extend it frequently and freely.

Make a conscious choice right now to forgive people who have hurt you in the past. Determine in your heart that you will make every effort to forgive those who will hurt you in the future. That is what God did concerning us. He knew we would screw things up, so He had a plan of reconciliation already in place.

A broken relationship that is repaired by forgiveness often becomes better than before. Keep in mind that the words you will write are an overflow of what is in your heart. Bitterness will spring forth in your work if you do not forgive. Forgiveness is essential to being a clean stream for the Father to flow through.

Therefore I say to you, her sins, which are many, are forgiven, for she loved much. But to whom little is forgiven, the same loves little. Luke 7:47 NKJV

"Better than Before"

Because of sin I searched my heart and my heart almost fainted.
Because of sin I searched my mind and my thoughts were so tainted.
Because of love I see no sin, I only see what is right.
Because of love I see no darkness, I only see the light.
Because of love a lamb was slain to take away our sin.
Because of love the lamb was sentenced before time began.
Because of grace, where sin abounds, grace abounds much more.
Because of Christ, God forgives our sins and makes things better than before.

Date: _____

Reflect on a time in which a friendship was mended through forgiveness.

Write the initials of someone you desire to be reconciled with.

Write the initials of a person that you do not see the need to be reconciled with. Pray for that person.

"Watch carefully that no one falls short of God's favor. That no well of bitterness springs up to trouble you and throw many others off the path."
Hebrews 12:15 VOICE

10. FIRST AID

"Getting over a painful experience is much like crossing monkey bars. You have to let go at some point in order to move forward."
-C.S. Lewis

After you have worked through offenses and made amends concerning a situation be very careful not to revisit the issue by dialoguing with others. A good rule of thumb is to treat a wound of offense the same way you would a wound on your body. Clean it and leave it alone so it can heal properly.

"The more you talk, the more likely you will cross the line and say the wrong thing; but if you are wise, you'll speak less and with restraint." Proverbs 10:19 VOICE

"Those who forgive faults foster love, but those who repeatedly recall them ruin relationships." Proverbs 17:9 VOICE

"Commit to Love"

I commit to love no matter how much hatred I see.
I commit to love because of Your love towards me.
I commit to love so grace will abound.
No matter how dark the night, love's light can be found.
Love that is patient, gentle and kind.
Love that suffers long, renewing the mind.
I can be meek because love is so strong.
I will let go because love remembers no wrong.
When prophecies knowledge and tongues all fail,
What is perfect will come and love will prevail.

First Aid

We are The Body of Christ, there are some similarities between how we heal emotionally and how we heal physically.

How to Treat a Flesh Wound

If the wound is bleeding severely, call 911.

FOR MINOR CUTS

Wash your hands with soap to avoid infection.

How to Treat a Wound of Offense

If the wound is bleeding severely, call on God.

FOR MINOR CUTS

Wash your hands of offenses, to prevent bitterness and hurt feelings.

Wash the cut thoroughly with mild soap and water to avoid infection

Use direct pressure to stop the bleeding.

If the cut is likely to get dirty or be re-opened by friction, cover it (once the bleeding has stopped) with a bandage that will not stick to the injury.

Call immediately for emergency medical assistance if:

The bleeding is severe, spurting, or cannot be stopped (for example, after 15 minutes of pressure).

The person is seriously injured.

Wash thoughts thoroughly with scripture to avoid condemnation.

Use immediate confrontation to stop confusion.

If the situation gets messy or re-opened by friction (gossip or contention), cover it in love.

Call on God immediately and Elders for spiritual assistance if:

The wound is severe or cannot be stopped (for example, gossip, jealousy, envy and discord).

If the person is seriously injured. (If someone's Salvation or sanity is at stake.)

Date: _____

The Body of Christ mirrors the human body. There are distinct similarities between the two, such as how a wound heals in the physical body versus how an emotional wound heals. In the same way that you would not amputate a limb because it has a flesh wound, we must be mindful to not cut a person completely out of our lives because they caused us an emotional wound. "Wounds inflicted by the correction of a friend prove he is faithful; the abundant kisses of an enemy show his lies." Proverbs 27:6 VOICE

Write about a time in which you cut off a friend because of a wound of offense.

Now reflect on a time in which someone you perceived as a foe was revealed to be a faithful friend.

It is easier to care for a wound than an amputation.

11. PLEADING THE 5TH

"Silence Speaks"

Today I sat in silence
And silence had something to say.
If you don't spend more time with me
You will cast your confidence away.
When many words are present
Regret is very near.
Draw close to me my child
And incline your ears to hear.
Always be slow to speak
And from many words refrain.
Rest in my presence
And I will keep you from causing pain,
I will grant you wisdom and help you cherish your days.
Even fools are perceived as wise
When they grow familiar with my ways,
I sat there in silence as silence spoke with me.
The truth spoken by silence...
Silently, set me free.

Date: _____

Reflect on a time in which silence set you free or when your silence spoke volumes.

Read Proverbs 17:28

Write a statement about silence.

"Silence can often be misinterpreted, but never misquoted."
-Author Unknown

12. ACCUSATIONS

You might be thinking to yourself, "Easy for you to say, but you don't know what I've been through. You don't know how people have lied on me and made all kinds of false accusations about me." I may not know, but God does and His word is very clear concerning what we should do when we find ourselves facing tough battles.

Since we are not fighting against flesh and blood, standing firm on God's word and suiting up daily in our spiritual armor are our best offensive weapons to combat the devil's schemes. Satan's express purpose in the earth is to accuse you. It should come as no surprise that he would try to convince you that everyone you meet is out to do the same.

"Moses told the people, Fear not; stand still (firm, confident, undismayed) and see the salvation of the Lord which He will work for you today. For the Egyptians you have seen today you shall never see again."

"The Lord will fight for you, and you shall hold your peace and remain at rest." Exodus 12:13 & 14 AMP

"Pride must die in you, or nothing of Heaven can live in you."
-Andrew Murray

Date: _____

Stop right there and read Ephesians 6:10-17
Trust in God's Word daily to refute the enemy's lies.
Tell your story in your own words so that the enemy's accusations hold very little weight.

And they overcame him by the blood of the Lamb and the word of their testimony. And they did not love their lives to the death.
Revelation 12:11 NKJV

13. FOR YOUR GOOD

Do you love the Lord? Are you called according to His purpose? Then what are you worried about? God needs warriors, not worriers. If you were in a fight with someone and you already knew the outcome of the fight was in your favor, would you worry about losing? Of course not. Why do you think people trash talk their opponent in boxing or during a sports game? To get in their head and make them second guess themselves. Do not dialogue with a defeated foe, he will only delight in your demise.

"In The End You Win"

When fighting against the enemy of your soul,
It is important to remember that he is a defeated foe.
The battle is already won and though it is far from done,
In the end, you win.
I will say it again.
In the end, you win.
Though you might wonder "when?"
Just be certain of one thing.
In the end, YOU WIN!

You might be down, but you are not out. God has the last word and His word says, in the end, you win!

"We are confident that God is able to orchestrate everything to work toward something good and beautiful when we love Him and accept His invitation to live according to His plan." Romans 8:28 VOICE

Date: _____

What is something you would do if you knew you would not fail?

If it is motivated by your love for God and He has called you to do it, stop focusing on everything that could go wrong, and trust God to make it right.

Setbacks, sorrow, sickness and suffering can be a setup for success.

14. WRITE IN THE DARK

In the beginning when the earth was dark and without form what did God do? He created. The information I am sharing was written during some of my darkest moments. Times in which there is a void can be some of your greatest times to create. Do not despise your humble beginnings. Do not discard the things you write during seasons when you are most vulnerable. It is my prayer that you look at your work and declare "That's good."

"It is a GOOD thing that I have been humbled because it helped me learn your limits. Your teachings are more valuable to me than a fortune in gold and silver."
Psalm 119: 71 & 72 VOICE

"Unto you this Life I Give"

When I am broken, cracked and all poured out.
I long for Your embrace.
When my mind is filled with fear and doubt.
I will run this race.
You died for me to live this life.
I appreciate Your sacrifice.
You were nailed, beat, bruised and torn.
I dare not complain about life's thorns.
Let foolish things confound the wise.
May Your word be true and every man a lie.
If I must die for You to live,
Then unto You this life I give.

Date _____

Write about a time in your life in which a breakdown led to a breakthrough.

Truly if God lives in you, He is greater than any difficulty you will ever face. Live in such a way that the light within radiates even in your darkest hour.

15. MINDFUL OF MAN OR MINDFUL OF GOD?

"Be who you are and say what you feel because those who mind don't matter and those who matter don't mind."
-Dr. Seuss

God created you in His image and likeness. It is safe to say that He created you the way He did for a purpose. Let me be clear, as long as you are not perverting His original design, there is an attribute of himself that He'd like to display through you in the earth. Sadly, some of the world's most creative minds have become so confused that they exchanged the truth of God for a lie and decided to worship and serve the creature rather than the Creator.

Being who you are in Christ can be a challenge because daily we are bombarded with invitations to be like or look like someone else. This can make you feel like you must apologize for thinking your own thoughts and feeling your own feelings. You may start to look foreign to those around you when you begin to live life from the inside out. Remember, heaven is your home and you were not designed to fit the pattern of this world. Being set apart is not bad if it helps you become familiar with what is on the inside; that is what matters most.

Caring too much about what man thinks is demonic. When we become self-conscious, it makes it difficult to remain God conscious. This may sound oxymoronic, but sometimes we have to care enough, to not care at all. Pay attention to what Jesus says to Peter in the following passage.

..."Get behind Me, Satan! For you are not mindful of the things of God, but the things of men." Mark 8:33 NKJV

Being direct can help us make moves in the right direction.
STAY FOCUSED

Date: _____

Look up John 15:9-11, Romans 12:2 & Psalm 27:1

Based on the above 3 scriptures, write a declaration to stay true to your divine design below.

Is there someone in your life that hinders you from being you? Feel free to grab a sheet of paper and write them a letter. Often times after I have done this exercise, I realize that it is not the person who is trying to change me, it is my perception of what I think that person thinks of me, that pressures me to conform.

16. UNCOMMON SENSE

The word of God is becoming less accepted in today's culture. However, it is the only thing that makes sense out of the nonsense that surrounds us each day. God's word brings clarity to confusion, breathes life back into dead things and causes us to triumph over and over trials. Build yourself up daily in the word. The Gospel is good news! Although it may be uncommon to hear the word spoken, speak it over yourself daily and deliberately. It will strengthen and establish you when you need it most.

"After you have suffered for a little while, the God of grace who has called you [to His everlasting presence] through Jesus the Anointed will restore you, support you, strengthen you, and ground you."
I Peter 5:10 VOICE

"The word of God, you see, is alive and moving; sharper than a double-edged sword; piercing the divide between soul and spirit, joints and marrow; able to judge the thoughts and will of the heart."
Hebrews 4:12 VOICE

People who do not have a personal relationship with Jesus tend to view Christians as being brainwashed. To some degree it is true. We are to daily wash our brains with God's word.

47

"This hope, which is a safe and secure anchor for our whole being, enters the sanctuary behind the curtain."

Hebrews 6:19 CEB

Date _____

Take a moment to write some of your favorite "go to" scriptures.

Share briefly why these scriptures have become an anchor for your soul?

Hebrews 6:19, refers to "hope" as an anchor for our souls. What does an anchor do exactly? It goes down deep into the water to bring stability. Hope is an anchor that reaches up to Heaven to do the same.

17. New Eyes

Surround yourself with eagles if you wish to soar. Take a look at who you are surrounded by if you would like to get a glimpse of where you are going. Sometimes it helps to be seen through new eyes.

New eyes focus. Old eyes roll.
New eyes liberate. Old eyes control.
New eyes turn away. Old eyes stare.
New eyes soften. Old eyes glare.
New eyes open wide. Old eyes sneer.
New eyes see in faith. Old eyes squint in fear.

There have been crossroads in my life in which God sent a pair of new eyes to help me recognize an attribute that I myself might have overlooked. I will never forget the day my son put on his first pair of glasses. He said, "Mom the trees have leaves!" "What did they look like to you before?" I asked." "Fuzz," he replied. It made my heart sad to think about all the beauty he had missed because he could not see clearly. My son is a great student who takes education seriously. For a year prior he had been telling me that it was hard for him to see the board. Neither Melvin nor I wear glasses so the thought never crossed my mind that he could not see the board because of impaired vision.

My perception was my reality and no matter how much I listened to him complain I could not understand his struggle. I think God can use a new friendship to help us see with greater clarity in the same way glasses corrected my son's vision. New friendships can help you recognize things that are hidden in plain sight and remind you of the hope that God has in store for your future.

Date: _____

Is there a local Writer's Guild, Focus Group, Think Tank, or online forum that you would benefit from joining?

Perhaps there is a blog you enjoy following. If so, do so. If not, maybe God is calling you to start something.

Jot down ideas of future groups you would like to join or start to gain a new vantage point that would place you in the presence of new eyes.

"Plans fall apart without proper advice; but with the right guidance, they come together nicely." Proverbs 12:22 VOICE

18. BE CHILDLIKE NOT CHILDISH

"No one can make you inferior without your consent."
-Eleanor Roosevelt

There have been times when I have felt childish for loving deep and forgiving quickly. Jesus had a special place for children in His heart. I wonder if it is because they love deep and forgive fast. Loving deep and forgiving freely is not childish, it is childlike.

Once while walking through repeat offenses with an individual, I cried out to the Lord and said, "Why does this person insult me and make me feel like a child?" I quietly heard the Holy Spirit whisper, "Unless you become as a little child you will not inherit the kingdom."

If there is someone in your life who has taken on the role of "self-appointed mentor" and treats you as if your childlike wonder is foolish and weak in contrast to their strength and wisdom, rest in knowing that God has a way of bringing things full circle. Do not allow someone else's hurting heart to hinder you from pursuing Jesus. That person will learn far more from your weakness than you will from their strength.

"But celebrate this: God selected the worlds foolish to bring shame upon those who think they are wise; likewise, He selected the world's weak to bring disgrace upon those who think they are strong." I Corinthians 1:27 VOICE

I have found that incredible writers and actors are also gifted teachers, but their strength usually lies in the fact that they are not afraid to be weak. Their vulnerability and transparency is what draws the reader or viewer in. There is a childlike wonder to every creative Christian. Chapter 3 verse 1 of James cautions Jewish Christians by saying, "Not many of you should become teachers..." His audience believed they could be justified through works of the law. If the main reason for wanting to be a writer is so that you can be the "teacher" and spiritually bully others, allow me to remind you of Paul's words. "When I was a child, I spoke, thought, and reasoned in childlike ways as we all do. But when I became a man, I left my childish ways behind." I Corinthians 13:11 VOICE

If someone has appointed themselves as a leader over you, know that God has creative ways of exposing pride and confounding human strength. Simply live your life in a way that no flesh can glory. It is not your job to prove to someone else how much wisdom you have or how strong you are. Be careful, lest you find yourself guilty of the very thing that is being done to you. Satan wants you to be childish instead of childlike.

"Who in your community is understanding and wise? Let his example, which is marked by wisdom and gentleness, blaze a trail for others. If your heart is one that bleeds dark streams of jealousy and selfishness, do not be so proud that you ignore your depraved state. The wisdom of this world should never be mistaken for heavenly wisdom; it originates below in the earthly realms, with the demons. Any place where you find jealousy and selfish ambition, you will discover chaos and evil thriving under its rule. Heavenly wisdom centers on purity, peace, gentleness, deference, mercy, and other good fruits untainted by hypocrisy. The seed that flowers into righteousness will always be planted in peace by those who embrace peace." James 3:13 VOICE

19. ALL POURED OUT

God can use our emptiness to fill others up. During one of my most overwhelming seasons of life, I began having women come to my house during my children's nap time. A time in which I felt so depleted God used me to pour into others. Being all poured out puts us in a perfect position for God to pour into us.

"When you go through deep waters and great trouble, I will be with you. When you go through rivers of difficulty, you will not drown! When you walk through the fire of oppression, you will not be burned up—the flames will not consume you." Isaiah 43:2 VOICE

"If you make sure that the hungry and oppressed have all that they need, then your light will shine in the darkness, and even your bleakest moments will be bright as a clear day." Isaiah 58:10 VOICE

"You spread out a table before me, provisions in the midst of attack from my enemies; You care for all my needs, anointing my head with soothing, fragrant oil, filling my cup again and again with Your grace." Psalm 23:5 VOICE

Jesus: "Blessed are the spiritually poor—the kingdom of heaven is theirs.

Blessed are those who mourn—they will be comforted.

Blessed are the meek and gentle—they will inherit the earth.

Blessed are those who hunger and thirst for righteousness

—they will be filled.

Blessed are the merciful—they will be shown mercy.

Blessed are those who are pure in heart—they will see God.

Blessed are the peacemakers—they will be called children of God.

Blessed are those who are persecuted because of righteousness—the kingdom of heaven is theirs.

And blessed are you, blessed are all of you, when people persecute you or denigrate you or despise you or tell lies about you on My account. But when this happens, rejoice. Be glad. Remember that God's prophets have been persecuted in the past. And know that in heaven, you have a great reward."

Matthew 5:3-2 VOICE

Date: _____

Read Matthew 5:3-12

Why would Jesus say that any one of those positions was a blessed one?

Notice that every area in which Christ considers us blessed is one in which our society would consider us to be deficient. Being empty is a perfect position for God to fill us up with Himself.

Who do you pour into?

Who pours into you when you are empty?

When we feel caught between a rock and a hard place is where we experience God's greatest comfort.

Praise God, the Father of our Lord Jesus Christ! The Father is a merciful God, who always gives us comfort. He comforts us when we are in trouble, so that we can share that same comfort with others in trouble. We share in the terrible sufferings of Christ, but also in the wonderful comfort he gives.

2 Corinthians 1:3-5 CEV

20. CONDEMNATION

"Beloved, if our heart does not condemn us, we have confidence toward God. And whatever we ask we receive from Him, because we keep His commandments and do those things that are pleasing in His sight." I John 3:21 & 22 NKJV

"Love Me Like You Do"

My best is never good enough, so what is there left to give?
Inadequate and insufficient is not the way to live.
I will never measure up to the standards of this world.
All I will ever be is this broken little girl.
I give and give and give some more and still it is not enough.
I pray and pray and pray some more and the battle is still tough.
I cry and cry until I am weak and it never makes me strong.
No matter how much I try to do right I am reminded that I am wrong.
But You, You love me. Brokenness and all.
You appreciate my fragments and pick up the pieces as they fall.
I don't know how you do it over and over again.
You look at me with eyes of love and erase my ugly sin.
Thank you for loving me though I feel so unworthy.
Thank you for cleansing me when I feel so dirty.
You restore and refresh me. You make all things new.
I could detest me and you would still love me like you do.

"There is therefore now no condemnation to those who are in Christ Jesus, who do not walk according to the flesh, but according to the Spirit. For the law of the Spirit of life in Christ Jesus has made me free from the law of sin and death." Romans 8:1 & 2 NKJV

God loves you even when you struggle with loving yourself.

59

Date: _____

Do you know what Romans 8:31 means? It means that you are forgiven, no longer guilty, will not receive punishment, no longer disapproved of. You are pardoned, set free, exonerated, accepted... Do you see the contrast between being condemned and being a conqueror?

Imagine the Holy Spirit as God's personal assistant. It comforts you and reveals truth that makes you free. Self-condemnation is like you becoming the enemy's personal assistant. Do you enjoy the thought of arming the enemy of your soul with ammunition to accuse you? Instead of rehearsing what the enemy says about you, take the time to recite God's word and rehearse truth that makes you free.

How do you recognize condemnation in your life?

How do you break free from it?

Allow the Holy Spirit to set you free by fully embracing all that grace has to offer.

"You see, God takes all our crimes—our seemingly inexhaustible sins—and removes them.
As far as east is from the west, He removes them from us."
Psalm 103:12 VOICE

We serve a God who takes away our inexhaustible sins and replaces it with inexhaustible grace.

21. FREE

Free yourself from wondering what might have been. Free yourself from wondering what people will think of you. Free yourself from the shame of your past. Free yourself of the fears that attempt to override your faith. Free yourself from trying to earn what Christ already paid the highest price for. Salvation is a gift, it's free! When Christ said, "It is finished", your freedom was paid for. You have been ransomed so that you could be set free from sin. If you were taken captive by a serial killer who said you could buy back your freedom at a high cost and someone volunteered to pay that cost would you pattern your life after the serial killer or the one who set you free? Satan has been stealing, killing and destroying for years; he is a sick and twisted serial killer. Thank God that our redeemer lives and that He purchased our freedom once and for all.

"Free"

Let faith arise and enemies scatter.
My heart will not faint
Though dreams have shattered.
I used to live this life for me,
Until He came and set me free.
I will fight this fight and finish strong.
I will worship God within the throng.
He has a perfect plan for me.
This awesome God who set me free.
He said, "Arise." He revealed my worth.
He called my name. He said, "Come forth."
He took my shame and gave me peace.
This Mighty God who set me free.
What can I do to repay this King?
The One who gave His everything.
He said, "Just live your life for me,
My love for you is free."

Date: _____

What have you been set free from? Write a Declaration of Freedom. Whenever you waver in your thoughts, meditate on your Declaration of Freedom.

"So stand strong for our freedom! The Anointed One freed us so we wouldn't spend one more day under the yoke of slavery, trapped under the law." Galatians 5:1 VOICE

22. HIDE AND GO SEEK

One of my favorite games as a child was "Hide and Go Seek." As Believers we "hide" (in Christ) and go "seek" The Father (In Heaven). A life hidden in Christ has advantages. American Church culture tends to associate visibility with productivity when often the inverse is true. Even though the person who is most visible may appear to be the most successful, it is often those hidden hands behind the scenes that are holding everything together. When the enemy tries his hardest to convince you that you have nothing to offer is when your life actually holds the greatest value. Do not shy away from a season in which you are hidden, be aware of the times that you wish to be seen.

HIDE
"Stay focused on what's above, not on earthly things, because your old life is dead and gone. Your new life is now hidden, enmeshed with the Anointed who is in God."
Colossians 3:2 VOICE

SEEK
"Seek first the Kingdom of God and His righteousness, and then all these things will be given to you too. So do not worry about tomorrow. Let tomorrow worry about itself. Living faithfully is a large enough task for today."
Matthew 6:33 VOICE

Hide and go seek was a game we once played.
Now it's a strategy to chase cares away.
When life fills with stress and your mind will not rest
Just start to count and begin your quest.
Seek first the kingdom and His righteous ways.
Count it all joy all of your days.
Trust in the Lord with all your heart.
See every end as a new start.
His grace is enough,
His word is still true.
It will work for your good
In the end when it's through.

Date: _____

Once I was walking through something and contacted a woman of wisdom. I felt like I was in a period of isolation. After she listened to my heart she said, "Toya, I don't think you are in a place of isolation. It sounds more like incubation." Sometimes God will conceal us to keep us from getting infected so that we can heal and grow stronger. Explore the lives of leaders like David, Moses and Joseph. Their character was developed during hidden years. Even Jesus had a time in which He was hidden. During that time He grew in stature and wisdom. If God appoints a hidden season in your life, take the time to do the same (grow in wisdom and stature). Remember, sometimes God hides us so that He can heal us.

How do you currently hide and go seek?

Social Media Fast
Stay at Home Day
Self-Planning Day
Vacation
Sabbatical
Turning your ringer off on your phone

Reflect on a time in which you experienced either isolation or incubation.

23. Pansies

Trust God's timing. Wait for your season. Some plants bloom when it is cold, others while it is hot. Some, once they have received enough water and others when they are buried deep in the soil. Some writers write in the winter seasons of life, others from a warm place; still others, go through dirt and manure. What is most important is that they write. Regardless of when, just rest in knowing that you will, and that everything you need is within. God is a Master Gardener. People may encourage you to write. Great leaders may water your gift, but ultimately, it is up to God to make you grow.

"My job was to plant the seed, and Apollos was called to water it. Any growth comes from God, so the ones who water and plant have nothing to brag about. God, who causes the growth, is the only One who matters."
I Corinthians 3:6 & 7 VOICE

Like pansies in the winter time
  Through hardened soil I seek sunshine.
  I often wonder "am I slow?"
  My maker says, "No, it takes time to grow."
  In summertime when all is in bloom.
  He gently whispers "still too soon."
  You will blossom when it's your season.
  At the right time for the right reason.
  Admitting, I don't quite understand,
  I do so trust His sovereign plan.
  I wait on Him to water me,
  He sees the roots I cannot see.
  He knows of blossoms that are yet to grow.
  He possesses knowledge I have yet to know.
  I will wait expectantly,
  Because all I need is within the seed.
  Time, water and determination
  Are additional factors in my cultivation.
  Someday I'll know His awesome power
  As I blossom into a fragrant flower.

Date _____

Have you ever seen pansies bloom in the winter? If you can remember, reflect on how you felt to see such a sight?

Did it warm your heart?

Did it bring you joy?

Were you green with envy?

Did hope deferred make your heart sad?

Were you angry with God?

Being envious, saddened or angry with a flower for doing what God designed it to do would be silly. God's creativity at work in the lives of others should inspire us. There is something captivating about the contrast between a pansy's vibrant color and the cold temperature. There should be something equally fascinating when a person blossoms in a winter season. We should celebrate their growth and be reminded that God is a Master Gardener and He will be faithful to cultivate the seeds He has sown in our hearts. That person did not wake up that day and say "Today is the day I will break through the soil." The seed within them was sown months or years prior. They simply bloomed when it was time. There is no reason to be jealous of someone else's growth.

Don't rush your process. God's timing is perfect.

"The same One who has put seed into the hands of the sower and brought bread to fill our stomachs will provide and multiply the resources you invest and produce an abundant harvest from your righteous actions. You will be made rich in everything so that your generosity will spill over in every direction. Through us your generosity is at work inspiring praise and thanksgiving to God. For this mission will do more than bring food and water to fellow believers in need—it will overflow in a cascade of praises and thanksgivings for our God." 2 Corinthians 9:10-12 VOICE

24. OVERSHARING

Oxford Dictionary defines oversharing as "revealing an inappropriate amount of detail about one's personal life."

I want to be very careful in approaching this topic because I don't wish for my words to create an environment in which you are walking on eggshells. Your testimony is yours to share and you are free to do so however you please. Allow me to offer a few concerns when it comes to the possibility of oversharing your story. In my understanding I would define oversharing as when you share your testimony in a way that leaves you or your listening audience feeling as though you just exposed your private parts in a public place. (This example demonstrates oversharing.) I have done it before and if it was as awkward as it was for me, I can only imagine how uncomfortable it was for the reader or listening audience. My goal is to encourage you to allow redemption and grace and to be the thread that holds the tapestry of your testimony together so that you can be spared of shame. The greatest way to do this is to look to God for guidance concerning what to share and when.

I am not saying these things to silence you. I want you to find your voice and I want your voice to be heard. Listen closely to the voice of the Lord as you share. In the Miranda Rights, it states "anything you say can be used against you in a court of law." Sometimes it is ok to exercise your right to remain silent. Allow the Holy Spirit to reveal truth to you. Even the most powerful testimony can lack effectiveness if it is shared without discretion.

Be mindful to resist succumbing to the peer pressure of sharing something that God has not released you to share yet. When it is time to share your full story, you will know. No one, but God, can determine that for you.

"Today I will Twirl"

Pain will not paralyze me because grace empowers me.
I will spin around and laugh from a pure place regardless of the
Fear and pollution that surrounds me.
My robe of righteousness will dance as I spin.
I will open my mouth wide to let the light in.
I will laugh and sing as I choose to be free.
Today I will twirl because I've been redeemed.
Full circle with warm fuzzies.
I will twirl 'til I fall and when I stand up
A new name I'll be called.
Forgiven, restored, renewed and refreshed.
I will offer my best & He'll do the rest.
Strength for weakness beauty for ash.
A future, a hope no more shame from my past.
I'll laugh 'til I cry the happiest tears because
I've been made new saved from all fear.
Today I will twirl!

4 Questions to Help Prevent Oversharing

1. Is this story mine to tell?
2. Can I tell it without exposing others in the process?
3. What is the age range of my listening audience?
4. Am I sharing what God wants me to say or what I think man wants to hear?

25. DON'T BITE

God told Adam and Eve all that they could enjoy in the garden and yet they took a bite out of the one thing He told them not to touch. Fitly spoken and well written words are like a lush garden. Don't bite off of forbidden fruit. Make it your aim to exercise integrity while writing. Cite sources when quoting someone.
Resist the temptation to nibble off the fruit of other people's labor. The enemy would like nothing more than to discredit your voice as a Christian Author.

PLEASURE
"All the things the world can offer to you—the allure of pleasure, the passion to have things, and the pompous sense of superiority—do not come from the Father. These are the rotten fruits of this world."
I John 2:16 VOICE

PRIDE
"Your heart swelled with pride because of your beauty and talents. Your hunger for fame, your thirst for glory corrupted your wisdom. This is why I drove you to the ground
and made an example out of you before a company of kings."
Ezekiel 28:17 VOICE

PROMOTION
There is a fine line between promoting the things we are passionate about and propagating pride. I pray that of all the places our gifts and talents permit us to go that we would desire to "go low" (humbly) and trust God to exalt us at the appointed time.

"The Latin "Word Plagiarius has many meanings, mainly "kidnapper, plagiarist."

Plagiarism "the act of using another person's words or ideas without giving credit to that person: the act of plagiarizing something."

Producing new ideas can feel like pregnancy. If you have ever had your words or ideas shared without your permission or acknowledgement, then you have experienced a kidnapping. I have six children and I cannot imagine how devastating it would be for someone to kidnap one of them. Imagine the effect it would have on our family, friends and entire community. The grief alone would be too much to bear.

I would want my child's face on every milk carton, newspaper, billboard, and all over social media. If I knew who the kidnapper was, I would want their face and name on every local news station, radio broadcast, plastered over the internet and would not relent until they were found and returned my child safe and sound.

To illustrate this on an even deeper level, imagine what it would feel like if you turned on the TV and saw a news clip of someone being honored with an award for raising a child with your likeness. You look closer and know for certain that is your child and someone else is being publicly praised for a child they privately stole from you.

There is a plague of plagiarism that is taking place in our world that daily goes unnoticed. Think about some ways you can safeguard yourself against plagiarism.

Practice making notes in your journal when you are quoting

someone else. Trusting God to give you His best and offer you fresh produce for your writing process. For more information on Plagiarism visit www.plagiarism.org

26. THE SECURITY OF PURITY

Define Security:
: The state of being protected or safe from harm
: Things done to make people or places safe

Define Purity:
: Lack of dirty or harmful substances
: Lack of guilt or evil thoughts

Remain pure so that you can write from a pure place. The more pure the root is, the more potent the fruit is. If you are pure in heart, you will yield fruit of importance. This fruit will in turn reproduce after its own kind. If you are bitter and hold grudges, you may find yourself living a life of impotence (barren, fruitless, sterile, infertile, unfruitful) rather than importance. Purity is secure. Contamination can create chaos. Write like your life depends on it because it does.

"Words kill, words give life;
they're either poison or fruit—you choose."
Proverbs 18:21 MSG

"Listen: to those who are pure, all things are pure. But to those who are tainted, stained, and unbelieving, nothing is pure because their minds and their consciences are polluted. They claim, "I know God," but their actions are a slap to His face. They are wretched, disobedient, and useless to any worthwhile cause."
Titus 1:15 VOICE

Words can bring death or life!

Talk too much, and you will eat everything you say.

Proverbs 18:21 CEV

27. Faith vs Fear

Biblestudy.com defines Mephibosheth in 2 ways.
1. Exterminator of shame; i.e., of idols.
2. out of my mouth proceeds reproach

You may be wondering, "What does this odd name have to do with me?" Everything. Mephibosheth's story is an example of how fear can cripple us or even those God has entrusted into our care.

Read the story of Mephibosheth.

2 Samuel 4:4

2 Samuel 9

2 Samuel 19:26-30

If his nurse would have been walking by faith instead of running in fear Mephibosheth would not have been crippled. Had she understood that David was coming to bestow kindness upon Mephibosheth she would have greeted the King with reverence rather than running away. This is symbolic of how many Believers have a misunderstanding of God. He sent Jesus to bestow kindness upon us and we live our lives running from a Savior that came to bless us.

Even after Mephibosheth was seated in the presence of the King, he still perceived himself as a dead dog. How do you perceive yourself? Someone who has received the gift of righteousness and can now walk by faith in right standing with God knowing confidently that you have been forgiven? Or one who only sees yourself as lame, crippled by the fall (of creation) weighed down by sin?

Some believers focus on sin; others focus on righteousness. Some live life walking by faith. Others live lives paralyzed by fear. Ziba tried to deceive King David concerning Mephibosheth in the same way that Satan accuses us before God and tries to steal the inheritance that Christ came to bless us with (the gift of righteousness). I love that Mephibosheth's confession in 2 Samuel 19:30 when he says he would rather see the King at peace rather than to share the land with Ziba. Do you have a similar conviction? Would you rather have the Prince of Peace reign in your heart than to have fortune and fame?

Are you starting to see what Mephibosheth has to do with you? Based on your perception you will either be one who scatters shame or one who eradicates it. Which one will you be?

28. RUN YOUR RACE DIY

Sometimes we all need strength for the journey to keep pressing toward the mark? This exercise may seem silly now but someday when you need it most, you will be thankful you took the time out to do it. Write yourself a letter. Here is an example of a letter I wrote to myself back in 2009. It still encourages me today.

Dear Toya,

Thank you for learning to live life in the moment; letting go of what's behind, not focusing on what's to come, but embracing the present. Enjoying each day as it has been given to you, knowing that God's grace is sufficient. Thank you for letting go of your legalistic ways and embracing grace that brings freedom and refreshment. I really enjoy your company, glean from your wisdom and have fun spending time with you.

Never forget how much God loves you. It shines through you in the way you love others. The more you pour out, the more He replenishes you. I can't help but to give God glory when I see your light shine before others. I admire the peace you walk in, it reflects how your mind is fixated on the Lord. I've watched the way you delight yourself in Him and He gives you the desires of your heart. God's strength is perfected in your weakness. You provoke me to dream bigger dreams. When I think about all that God has done in your life, it makes me look forward to the hope and the future that He has for me.

Thank you for being obedient. Breaking free from what men think and holding fast to the things of God. I know this road has not been an easy one. It is nice to know that God always causes you to triumph and works things out for your good. When you speak of His love it makes me want to know Him more. When He reveals a new truth to you it blesses me to see your zeal and reception. Do not let anyone look down on you because you are young. Keep setting an example before others. Continue to run hard after Him and don't let anything or anyone hinder you. He has good plans for you. He will perfect that which concerns you and will be faithful to complete the good work that he began in you. Continue to cast your cares upon Him, place your trust in Him and seek His kingdom first. No eye has seen, nor ear has heard what God has prepared for you. May mercy, peace, grace and love be yours in abundance.

Yours Truly,

Toya Poplar

PS. Remember, I Samuel 30:6 "...David encouraged himself."

The reason I titled this chapter, "Run Your Race DIY" is because no one can run your race for you. You have to "do it yourself." It may seem narcissistic at first to write a letter to yourself, but no one but you and God know what words of encouragement you need to hear. Imagine what it was like for the woman with the issue of blood to say over and over to herself, "If I could just touch the hem of his garment, I will be made whole." (Matthew 9:21) In the end her faith made her well. Her private struggle was so intense that she had no time to worry about what she looked like to the general public. It did not matter if she looked crazy muttering to herself as she pressed her way through the crowd, all that mattered was in the end, she was healed.

29. Self-Care

"Self," independent from God is deceitful, wicked & should be denied; most of us are aware of that. But there is an urgent need for Self-Care within the Body of Christ. As a matter of fact, Christians should be experts in Self Care.

"You should love the Eternal, your God, with all your heart, with all your soul, with all your mind, and with all your strength." The second great commandment is this: "Love others in the same way you love yourself." There are no commandments more important than these." Mark 12:30-31

How can we effectively love our neighbor if we do not love ourselves?

10 Self Care Tips

1. Hydration-drink water, it has so many benefits.
2. Rest-go to bed, be kind to your body and your brain.
3. Simplify-clutter kills creativity. Clean up.
4. Exercise-Get moving. Endorphins make you happy.
5. Love yourself well so that you can love others well.
6. Stay in the Word-renew your mind daily.
7. Stay Motivated-If you don't motivate you, who will?
8. Invest in your gift- do your best and God will do the rest.
9. Create-a vision board, trust me, they work.
10. Get Away-know when to retreat.

When you feel lost in the dark.

Psalm 27:1
The Lord is my LIGHT and my SALVATION-Whom shall I fear? The Lord is the stronghold of my life-of whom shall I be afraid?

When you feel all alone, like no one has your back, understands or even cares about you.

Duet. 31:8
The Lord Himself goes before you and will be with you; He will NEVER leave you nor forsake you.

When you feel hopeless, stuck, immature, like you just can't get it together.

Philippians 2:13
God is working in you, giving you the desire to obey Him and the POWER to do what pleases Him.

When you feel weak and helpless like you'll never finish.

Philippians 4:13
I can do EVERYTHING through Him who gives me STRENGTH.

When you are confused about what to do and you don't know where to turn.

James 1:5
If you want to know what God wants you to do ASK Him, and He will gladly tell you.

When your heart is downcast, deceitful and wicked.

Psalm 51:10
Create in me a PURE heart, O God and renew a STEADFAST spirit within me.

30. DAILY BREAD

Read Luke 24:13-35

Jesus appeared to two disciples after the crucifixion. He walked with them on a seven mile journey and they did not recognize who He was. We have all been there before, so downcast by our disappointment that we do not realize that our hope is hidden in plain sight. As they walked the road to Emmaus Jesus began at Moses and all the prophets explaining what took place. As they tried to bring Him up to speed on what had just taken place in the present, He reminded them of all that had happened in the past (concerning Himself). What a great example of what we are to do with our words. No matter what someone is facing we should always point people to Christ. When our own outcomes look grim and our understanding is darkened, we should look for Jesus.

Their hearts burned within them while they walked upon the road and listened to "The Word" talk about the Word. However, it was not until He broke bread that they were able to recognize Him for who He was. What do you notice about our Savior's leadership style from this passage of scripture? Our role is to point people to Christ and stay out of God's way. Jesus gave the disciples a reminder to REMEMBER Him. He opened their eyes, by opening the scriptures and it in turn opened their hearts. Their response was to go and share what they had experienced with those who were closest to them. That is the response we want people to have as they experience our creative efforts. That they would go share the good news of the gospel with others and make God's fame great in the earth. The enemy of our soul would like nothing more than for us to seek out fame for ourselves when our collective call is to point people towards Christ so that they can make God famous.

What was the result of the time they shared with the Savior? They were refreshed, energized and their joy was restored. When we spend time with The Word, our hearts burn within us, that fresh fire reminds us to see beyond our circumstances and look at the big picture. Notice that Jesus started with Moses and all the prophets working His way back to where they were. Never become so familiar with scripture that you fail to see it as fresh manna. There is a reason that Jesus taught us to pray, "Give us this day, our daily bread."

Date: _____

Why is Jesus referred to as "The Bread of Life?"

Write about ways in which you can be a wise teacher that shows people truth then steps out of the way?

31. EMPOWERED BY POWERLESSNESS

God does not despise our weakness. It only magnifies His strength. His grace is sufficient for us. When we feel helpless, He is a helper. When we feel unreliable, He is dependable. When we lack ability, He is well able. When we feel forsaken, He is most present. When we feel let down, He lifts us up. When we feel useless, He is most useful. When we feel less than, He is the greatest. When we feel unstable, He is our rock. When we feel lost, lied to and ready to die, He is the way, the truth and the life.

"Don't let the wise brag of their wisdom.
Don't let heroes brag of their exploits.
Don't let the rich brag of their riches.
If you brag, brag of this and this only:
That you understand and know me.
I'm God, and I act in loyal love.
I do what's right and set things right and fair,
and delight in those who do the same things.
These are my trademarks."
God's Decree. Jeremiah 9:23 MSG

Joseph had nothing and was called a success because the Lord was with him, Genesis 39:2. It is not about what you have, it is about Who you have. We have everything we need in Christ. Isn't it amazing that an all sufficient God would choose to use broken vessels to carry out His plans in the earth?

Think about all the times that brokenness has led to something beautiful. Life's problems become opportunities for great growth. If you can maintain the perspective that life is a tapestry and although all we see is threads and knots, God sees the front of this ornate cloth and someday we too will see His masterpiece. Choose to see what He sees. Jesus said it Himself, "I only do what I see my Father doing." John 5:19-20

86

Date: _____

How do you currently see God using either your past or present powerlessness to empower others?

CLOSING WORDS

Rather than educate you on how to write a book, allow me to encourage you to simply write. The best advice I have concerning how to write is to take it one word at a time. This very book that you are reading consists of several moments of inspiration woven together to make a tapestry that has collectively become *Stop Write There*.

My purpose for writing this book is to encourage you to be intentional about finding your voice, capturing what the Father is saying to you and what He would like to express through you. My desire is that you will in turn encourage others to do the same by entertaining them with your experiences or educating them with your insight.

Limitations, we all have them. What are yours?

"I do not have time to write."

It sounds like you need to start making time.

"If I take the time to write, I won't have time to read my Bible."

God is the author of time. He can create a moment in which time stands still or he can redeem the time.

"When I take time to write, it makes me get behind in work or ministry."

Your words are the only reflection of your life's work that will be left in the earth someday.

Will your grandchildren know the type of person you were by that neatly folded pile of laundry you just finished? Will your children remember the caliber parent you were by the way you conduct your board meetings? Your words, songs, plays, poetry and published works and private journals will tell readers more about you in one hour of than an entire lifetime of devotion to keeping a clean house or you being a top notch employee or CEO.

What would you like for them to remember most about you? Writing is a wonderful way to leave a legacy in your own words. What is most important to you; leaving a financial inheritance that could quite possibly corrupt their character, or a legacy of faith that can fortify them to weather life's storms?

We established earlier how faith can take you further than finances ever could. Scripture tells us that a wise man leaves an inheritance for his children's children. Have you ever read, "My Utmost for His Highest?" By Oswald Chambers or "Jesus Calling" by Sarah Young. Their labor of love is leaving a legacy of faith that the entire Body benefits from, as well as an inheritance for their families.

Sometimes the very assignment we avoid completing is the one that can lighten our load and lead to a life of fulfillment and blessing. The places you will go, the people you will meet and the doors of opportunity await you. The moments of introspection and documented growth are invaluable. Writing gives you the opportunity to someday reflect back on life and see that as a result of cultivating your craft others benefited from your going public with your personal relationship with Jesus Christ.

The right words at the right time have the power to heal, break bondages and set captives free. The first step to freeing others is to be free yourself. Allow your creative process to set you free. In order to do so, you must first be free to create.

Although *Stop Write There* is written as a guide to help Christian writers write from a pure place, the message is certainly not limited to writers. The principles and pointers shared applies to all relationships. If you are experiencing Writer's Block, or emotional blockage in friendships or your relationship with the Lord, then you are in a perfect position to stop right there and begin journaling your way to freedom with *Stop Write There*. In case you are wondering to yourself, "Why Journal?" Think of a situation in which you have been wounded. If you have contaminants in your heart when you prepare to write a sermon, book or song, you run the risk of polluting others. If you are not sure whether you have forgiven someone and are ready to move forward, pay attention to what comes out of your mouth. It is the best indicator of what is in our hearts.

FOR THE PASTORS

Are you in need of a reboot because you have too many windows open on the desktop of life? Does this poem sound like a cry from the quiet places of your heart?

"Control Alt Delete"

I'm under attack, what do I do?
I'm taken aback, in need of rescue.
Defending myself, a dangerous place.
In need of help, it shows on my face.
Clenching my teeth, about to snap.
Heart rate increased, stuck in a trap.
My hands are cold, my temper is hot.
About to unfold, stomach in knots.
Where do I run, no place to hide?
I am undone, fit to be tied.

I want to scream, I want to fight.
I'm holding my breath, I know it's not right.
How did I manage to arrive at this stage?
It's not my nature to be filled with such rage.
Where did this come from, this is not me?
Don't answer that, I don't want to see.

Time to exhale, take a deep breath.
Love will prevail, no time for death.
Time to forgive, time to let go.
It's time to live, it's time to grow.
You will mature, this too shall pass.
You must endure, this pain won't last.
I know it's trying, so was the cross.
Although you're crying, all is not lost.
Peace will surpass what you understand.
A snake on the ground is a staff in your hand.
You take the tail, let God take the lead.
Prayer will avail, Control, Alt, Delete.

Sometimes people are like computers; we overheat, get viruses and need a reboot? You are not alone. Maybe you are not there now but you have gone there in the past and now desire to be pre-emptive against a mental hard drive crash. Have you gone years without a "real" vacation? Have you given the better parts of yourself to nonprofit work and ministry and given your family your left overs?

Hyperextension is not healthy. As I said before, this journal was designed to motivate you to focus on what is left and not lament over what has been lost. If you are a leader that has poured out on a weekly basis for years, take a break. It is my prayer that with each page you have turned that there have been moments in which you felt like I hijacked your heart's journal and wrote my prompters based off your personal entries. God is the author of time and in His sovereignty He knew precisely when you would find yourself at this junction in life.

Years ago, my husband and I were deeply immersed in ministry and though we loved the people we ministered to dearly; we loved our family, health and sanity more. When life got crazy, we quit life. When life as we knew it became a thing of the past we tapped into life more abundantly. God took our household from a state of tremendous stress and translated us into a place of perpetual peace.

Once while vacationing we attended a compelling Timeshare presentation. We did not purchase the Timeshare but the salesman's pitch was the most powerful sermon I have ever heard preached. My husband and I walk into any presentation prepared for the usual Jedi Mind Tricks, but this salesman was unique. He genuinely spoke from the heart and it reached my heart. He shared truth in love and I could not deny that what he was saying was true. He disarmed our defenses by taking time to get to know each family represented and shared candid stories about his own family.

This was not your traditional Timeshare presentation. This was a model for what church should be like. The only way that salesman could speak from such an intimate place was because he had experienced what it is like to be on the brink of losing everything because he was previously so driven by work. There is not much difference between that salesperson and most pastors. The only difference is most pastors do not have the courage to admit where they are. Therefore, they remain frozen like a computer screen that has too many windows open at the same time.

I am not saying quit ministry forever, but I am saying, do not be afraid to take a Sabbatical so that you can reboot your heart, mind and approach to ministry. In the same way honor begets honor. Busyness begets busyness.

If your congregation feels like they are being driven,
It is probably because you are no longer being led.
If they feel like they are starving.
It is because you are no longer being fed.
If they feel like they are being talked at.
It is because you are not being talked to.
You can deny what they are feeling.
But God knows that it is true.

Do you feel like Moses? Has your congregation been going in circles for years? What did God want the children of Israel to do? To enter into His rest.

When you prepare Sunday's sermon, do you feel like Paul when he addressed the church at Corinth? Is there a lack of unity, morality and love in your congregation? I am sure you have seen your fair share of all of the above. What was Paul's most effective form of communicating God's heart to the church? It was through his letters. (Paul took the time to Stop Write There)

There is something special that takes place when we put words on paper. Science shows that we store information in a different portion of our brain when we have interaction of pen and paper. When was the last time that you wrote a letter? An actual real life letter to someone in your church family? Letter writing is like giving someone a piece of your heart and sadly it has become a lost art.

"And I, Paul—in my own handwriting!—send you my regards. If anyone won't love the Master, throw him out. Make room for the Master! Our Master Jesus has his arms wide open for you. And I love all of you in the Messiah, in Jesus." I Corinthians 16:21-24 MSG

There are some leaders that will read this and make room for the Master. There are others who may dismiss it and keep doing things the way they have always been done. Much like the timeshare salesman, I must ask you "What does it feel like when you see other church families enjoying their journey with Jesus, while the people in your congregation are busy backbiting, nagging, complaining and hurting one another?"

What caused the delay in the children of Israel reaching the Promised Land? Murmuring and complaining. Why did a whole generation not get to enter into the Promised Land? Because of their disobedience and unbelief. I am seeing the same trend take place in the body of Christ. While one generation murmurs, complains and longs for things to be the way they were back when they were in bondage; a new generation is laying hold of the promises of the good things that are to come. They are ready to relinquish the traditions of man that make the gospel of no effect. Which category does your congregation fall under?

Why can't a man put new wine into old wineskins?
They run the risk of losing them both. The new wine and the old wineskins. Do you have young people in your congregation that have an intimate relationship with Jesus that are on fire ready to do radical things for the kingdom of God? Do you have older people in your congregation who are holding fast to all things religious and spend more time demonizing everything that does not look like what their parents and grandparents did? If these questions are hitting close to home, my encouragement would be, do not throw the baby out with the bathwater, but do not drown the adult who ran the bathwater to begin with.

Find a way in which the voice of each generation can be heard. Start with recording your own voice, as well as what God is speaking to you presently. You will be amazed by how everyone under the sound of your voice each week will benefit from not hearing your voice temporarily so that you can all hear the voice of God clearly.

"Don't let anyone belittle you because you are young. Instead, show the faithful, young and old, an example of how to live: set the standard for how to talk, act, love, and be faithful and pure." I Timothy 4:12 VOICE

"Eternal One (to the people): Stand at the crossing, and consider the ancient path, for it is good and it leads to Me. Walk on this path, and you will find rest for your souls. But they have said, "We will not walk upon this road."
Jeremiah 6:16 VOICE

FOR THE PEOPLE

Are you tired of hearing regurgitated words? Different versions of the same thing. Are you starting to feel as though you spend more time reading your Bible than your pastor does? No disrespect to pastors but you probably do. I have compassion for pastors because they have so many people pulling on them. Ask yourself how can you lighten their load? What are you supplying to the body?

I look forward to the day that the church's focus shifts from building buildings, to building people. Just then I bet a particular congregation popped into your mind. I am not referring to them. I am referring to you, you are "The Church." It is time for us to stop competing and start creating safe places for people to dialogue. Most church environments have become a monologue.

In order for the church to truly thrive, we must find a way to create atmospheres in which people can talk with one another rather than at each other. I often joke about Bathroom Ministry and Parking Lot ministry. Sometimes those are the only places in which people actually get to speak with one another. Have you ever felt that the least of what you get from church takes place in the sanctuary?

People need people. As you serve in your local body be intentional about getting to know the people around you. Far too many people are like babies who die from lack of touch. Widows and orphans have something in common. There is no one there to touch them. Be the hands that reach out and touch the untouchable reach the unreachable, love the unlovable, embrace those who have been rejected. Stop asking questions like "What would Jesus do?" And do the stuff He did.

"What you've done to the least of them you've done unto me." (Matthew 25:40)

97

In the same way that you may feel as though you spend more time studying The Word than your pastor, you may also spend more time serving and ministering to people. Before you amen in agreement with me, allow me to paint a picture for you. Your Pastor has a staff, a board of directors, secretary, Associate Pastor, leadership team, Deacons, Elders, nursery workers, janitorial service, Ushers, Worship Team... And you have just you. Maybe you also have your spouse and your children. Look at all the helping hands your Pastor has that you do not. Set some boundaries and do so quickly. The chapters that you wish to write would be written if you would stop giving away pamphlets.

Sometimes all we need is permission. We are called to provoke one another unto love right? Well allow me to provoke you. If I can do it, you can too. You have always sensed in your heart that you were called to be an Author; let me encourage you to also be a Finisher.

God does not just start stuff. He finishes it. He does not just commence things. He completes them. Your life is a curriculum that others can learn from. Look at every failed attempt, dream deferred and divine delay as an opportunity for God to rewrite your story. Any good Author knows the power of brainstorming, writing an outline, a rough draft, revising and editing. No labor is in vain during the creative process. It all has a purpose. The Author has the authority to omit characters, change the scenery or even start from scratch. Let God be God. Even if at times it seems that He's suffering from writer's block, know Him today not just as The Author, But as The Finisher of your faith.

Then the Lord answered me and said:

"Write the vision

And make it plain on tablets,

That he may run who reads it.

For the vision is yet for an appointed time;

But at the end it will speak, and it will not lie.

Though it tarries, wait for it;

Because it will surely come,

It will not tarry.

Habakkuk 2:2-4

Author's Affirmation

I pray that your today is better than yesterday
That you will live life like tomorrow is not promised.
Today is all you have so do not squander it with worry.
May you embrace God's peace, trust His provision,
Receive His grace and be clothed in His righteousness.
Forgive quickly. Love deeply.
Speak truthfully and find joy in every circumstance.
May your life's soundtrack play a song of victory as you acknowledge the
Greater One who lives on the inside of you. Embrace change. Work hard.
Rest well. Cultivate growth
And own where you have dropped the ball.
God will pick up the pieces and fix your fragments
As you trust His sovereign plan.

"This brings me solace in the midst of my troubles: that Your word has revived me."

Psalm 119:50 VOICE

Trust in God's word no matter what!

If *Stop Write There* has helped you find a fresh start, get unstuck or simply inspired you to write, I would love to hear from you. My prayer for this journal is that it's ending would be your beginning. Keep in mind that success is not solely found in finishing, it is having the courage and faith to begin. Enjoy your journaling journey!

contact@stopwritethere.com

www.stopwritethere.com

NOTES

NOTES

ABOUT THE AUTHOR

Toya Poplar is a poet and speaker who enjoys being a conduit that helps others cultivate creativity and experience God intimately. Toya writes for a local publication and teaches journal writing to young ladies at a local Christian Academy. Married to her high school sweetheart rapper/engineer, Melvin "Proverbalist" Poplar; together they have 6 children, photograph weddings and host an accountability group for poets and rappers. When Toya is not preparing meals for her family, hanging out with her husband or photographing clients she spends her time cultivating sisterhood with friends.

IF YOU LIKED THIS BOOK...

- Share www.stopwritethere.com with your friends.

- Log onto Facebook.com/stopwritethere, click "LIKE" and post a comment regarding how you enjoyed your journaling journey.

- Tweet "I recommend reading #Stopwritethere @ToyaPoplar

- Hashtag: #Stopwritethere

REFERENCES

CHAPTER 26
http://www.merriam-webster.com/dictionary/plagiarism
"Security." *Merriam-Webster.com*. Merriam-Webster, n.d. Web. 5 Sept. 2015.
<http://www.merriam-webster.com/dictionary/security>.

"Purity." *Merriam-Webster.com*. Merriam-Webster, n.d. Web. 5 Sept. 2015.
<http://www.merriam-webster.com/dictionary/purity>.

"Impotent." Merriam-Webster.com. Merriam-Webster, n.d. Web. 5 Sept. 2015.
<http://www.merriam-webster.com/dictionary/impotent>.

CHAPTER 27
http://www.biblestudytools.com/dictionary/mephibosheth/

http://www.studylight.org/dictionaries/hbd/view.cgi?n=4223